CW00502133

CONTENTS

Special thanks to Rebecca Ramsey and Denise Robertson

Cover art by Bethany Perry

CHAPTER ONE

In this chapter I will explain the two levels of fear of weight gain as I see them, and explain how everyone has at least "Level One" fear of weight gain.

LEVEL ONE FEAR OF WEIGHT GAIN

IMPLICIT BIAS

I'm going to apologize in advance, because being told by someone you have implicit bias is inherently annoying. So yeah, sorry, but you do.

Implicit bias refers to the attitudes, ideas, and beliefs that form our understanding of the world, and therefore affect our actions, reactions, and decisions in an unconscious manner. These structural underpinnings of the way we see the world are largely subconscious, which is the very thing that makes them so very infuriating. When you are accused of having an unconscious or implicit bias, you feel like you are being told off for something you didn't do, because you don't know you are doing it. Which, in a sense, you are. It isn't your fault you have implicit bias. It was inflicted on you by the culture. You didn't choose it, but you are still very much impacted by it.

Most of you will be aware of the conversation surrounding implicit bias and race. The idea being that people who are not consciously or intentionally racist are still racist to a degree because so much of what we have been brought up to see as normal in the world is actually racially unequal. When I am referring to implicit bias, fear of weight gain and fatphobia, I'm getting at the same sort of thing.

I make a distinction between fear of weight gain and fatphobia. Fatphobia refers to the fear and dislike of fat people and the discriminatory behaviours and attitudes towards people in larger bodies. Fear of weight gain is about fearing gaining weight — for yourself or other people — and the subsequent restrictive behaviors you engage in or encourage others to engage in because you believe that doing so will prevent you gaining weight. Additionally, and rather oddly, many people with restrictive eating disorders like larger bodies and are even advocates for them — so long as they are someone else's body and not their own. So it is less of a discrimination against larger bodies in general, and more of an issue with their own body gaining weight. Fatphobia describes the fear and dislike of fat people and the stigmatization of individuals with bigger bodies. Fear of weight gain is more specifically a fear of putting on weight oneself.

Fear of weight gain is also sometimes a little odd in people with long-term restrictive eating disorders in that many of us get to the point where we want to be in our recovered body, and welcome it, but are afraid of the process of gaining weight and therefore struggle to take the actions of eating more and resting.

Level One fear of weight gain is something everyone in our culture has, because we live in a culture that is biased towards thinness. We live in a world that believes that thin is good and fat is not. It is both a conscious and an unconscious bias for many people. Everyone has it on some level, including our healthcare providers. In fact, they are often most affected by thin bias and fatphobia because the healthcare system, and therefore their schooling, reeks of it. The problem with a cultural bias is that nothing avoids being infected by it. If it is simply understood as a cultural "truth" that being fat is bad, then any scientific research that takes place is conducted by researchers who already have this bias. Rather like tasking the Vatican with researching whether God exists or not, you're just not going to get anything other than what the people doing the research already believe. There is no such thing as completely unbiased research because to be human is to be biased. The social nature of humans leads us to this fault — but cultural biases likely served to keep us safer and more connected with our neighbours in past times, so to label it a fault is somewhat ignorant too. Anyway, this isn't an anthropology book, so let's not get into all that.

In the field of eating disorder recovery especially, the bias towards thinness, and fear of weight gain is problematic in many healthcare providers. In my opinion, any person who treats people with eating disorders has to have done their own work around their own implicit biases to be at all useful to their patients. Any provider who hasn't is a liability, and that is currently most people in the field.

"Liability" may seem like a strong word to use, but I stand by it. I have lost count of the number of clients I have had who have been in treatment for a restrictive eating disorder and have been told to restrict their eating by a therapist or a dietitian because they began to gain weight. Even in treatment centers where people are sent for the purpose of gaining weight, the providers just can't help but get twitchy and nervous when weight gain actually starts to happen. That's because despite their role, they unconsciously have beliefs that weight gain is negative, and they have that default reaction to weight gain in their clients. Well, their clients pick up on it, even if it is subtle, and it does affect them. Even more so because the anxiety about their weight gain is coming from a "professional." In this sort of instance, more harm is done than good.

HOW DID YOUR IMPLICIT BIAS TOWARDS THINNESS START?

If you have fear of weight gain, which I am telling you that you do, how did you "get" it?

It started before you could speak. Highly likely it started before you could understand words.

Here's how:

Imagine you're a little tiny baby and you are sitting there in your nappy with your dummy in your mouth, and your mother and her friends are cooing over you. You don't know what they are saying because you are too young to understand words. However, your baby brain is paying attention — it pays attention to everything because it is preparing you for language, among other things. Your bright little eyes are tracking the faces of the people around you, and your sharp little ears are picking up on the sounds they are making. Some words that humans say you are beginning to recognise the sound of, because they are said frequently. Words like "hiya," and "mummy," and "bath." You may not know the words that the adults are saying in this conversation, but your brain (more specifically the language department of your brain) is at work. You are taking it all in, and your baby brain is frantically trying to piece together the puzzle of language.

Unfortunately, weight talk is highly prevalent in our culture among parents and peers both before and after giving birth. *"Losing the baby weight"* is a hot topic. But it's not just new parents who engage in diet talk; everyone does. For many people, talking about weight gain and weight loss is as common as talking about the weather.

Your baby brain starts to track words and sounds that your parents and their friends are saying. It begins to notice that some of the word sounds the adults make are accompanied with facial expressions and tone of voice that you have learned to associate with positive things, and some of the word sounds they make bring facial expressions and tone of voice that you have learned to associate with negative things. You are working out that facial expressions and tone of voice correlate with good and bad experiences. When your mother is talking to you, she smiles, the tone of her voice is higher, and her eyes look bright and happy. When she drops your bottle on the floor, she frowns, her tone of voice is lower, and she looks cross.

Your brain begins to notice the the word sounds *"weight loss"* are often accompanied with happier facial expressions and higher tone of voice. The words *"weight gain"* on the other hand, bring a lower tone of voice and frowning. Your baby brain begins to pick up that the word sound *"fat"* is often said in a low tone, accompanied with a facial expression that indicates it is unfavourable... Whereas *"thin"* seems to be associated with positive vibes.

That's just one example of your hyper-absorbant baby brain making sense of the world around it. Now imagine all of the other images, media, conversations, and observations that a baby will have before the age of two that will reinforce the idea that fat is bad and thin is good.

Kind of eye-opening to think of it like that, isn't it?

This is how implicit bias forms. Weight descrimination is so culturally normal that we are absorbing the concept of it before we can even understand words. This means by the time you are 5 years old, your brain has accepted it as a truth that weight gain is bad and weight loss is good. That fat is bad and thin is good.

Implicit bias is sneaky. It isn't as obvious as your parents sitting you down when you are three years old and giving you a lecture on the benefits of staying thin. It's not a class called *"How to be fat-phobic"* taught in school. It doesn't arrive in your life with a bang when on your fifteenth birthday. It's more like that old armchair that's always been there. It is understated and quiet, most of the time. Sure, every now and then it is more obvious — you usually become more aware of it when you are in your teenage years. Someone makes a comment like *"you're filling out,"* that feels like a slap in the face. I remember those very words being said to me when I was fourteen, and I remember feeling confused by them, as they were said as if I had done something wrong but I wasn't sure what. Until that day, it hadn't ever occurred to me that my body was anything other than perfect.

This was the first time someone had directly spoken to me about my developing and growing body as if it were an unfortunate blunder. Luckily for me, I was a confident enough kid that those words didn't cause me to worry, nor did they cause me to dislike my body. What I do remember feeling, however, was as if a concept that I had suspected was lurking below the surface had shown itself up more clearly. *Yes, I thought so, people think it is better to be thin.* When I brought this up with my best friend she looked at me as if I had two heads. *"Well, duh ... yeah gaining weight is bad. Everyone knows that!"*

And this is what I mean when I say that everyone in our culture has Level One fear of weight gain.

LEVEL TWO

"Level Two" describes the further and amplified fear of weight gain that happens when you develop a restrictive eating disorder. This is additional learning that weight gain is a threat over and above that of the implicit bias taught by our culture. This learning comes about as a result of your brain watching you consistently act in a way that is fearful and avoidant of weight gain. Basically, you start acting as if weight gain is a threat to you — by restricting, compulsively exercising, purging etc — and in doing so you massively strengthen your fear of weight gain.

Your brain doesn't stop learning about the world when you grow up. It never stops learning. However, once a belief system (such as the belief that thin is better than fat and that weight gain is undesirable) is established, your brain will pay particular attention to anything that reinforces that belief system. This is true of any belief system. If you believe in God, your brain is more likely to explain good things that happen as a miracle rather than serendipity. If you believe that the world is flat, your brain will seek out instances that confirm this. If you believe that vaccines cause autism, your brain will see correlates between vaccines and autism where others don't. Once a belief system has been established it is like your own personal echochamber in your head. But this echochamber has shelves, and it stores all the instances of things that confirm the already existing belief system as evidence. It is very backed-up when it comes to confirming data. That's why you should never argue with someone about religion or politics, and you will run out of breath before you will ever convince a flat-earther that our planet is round.

Our cultural implicit bias towards thinness predisposes our brains to be more likely to believe anything that reinforces the concept that weight gain is a negative thing. It also means we will be more likely to disbelieve or ignore anything that challenges this concept. Implicit bias is like the gift that keeps on giving in that sense: it puts a filter over your perception that weighs incoming data in favour of your already established belief system. I talked about perception a lot in *Rehabilitate, Rewire, Recover!* because understanding how your brain filters what is coming in via your senses is important if you want to try and achieve a more truthful picture of the world. When your brain believes that weight gain is bad or unhealthy, you view the world through that filter.

So ... you develop a restrictive eating disorder. This results in you beginning to *act* in a way that very much favours weight loss and avoids anything that might lead to weight gain. You restrict food. You maybe start exercising more. You might purge. You avoid eating higher-fat foods. You avoid foods that you consider "unhealthy." You don't eat as frequently as you truly want to. You stop responding to hunger signals promptly. You may do all or just a few of these things. It doesn't matter. All that matters is that you are behaving in a way that is avoidant of weight gain, and your brain is watching you do so and learning from it.

What is your brain learning from watching you act avoidant of weight gain? It is learning that weight gain must be a threat. If it wasn't a threat, why would you be going out of your way to avoid it?

Every single time you restrict or eat less than you truly want to, you give your brain another data point that says weight gain must be bad. Another item of "proof" to store in your personal echo-chamber's library. These data points pile up on top of your already existing Level One fear of weight gain and form Level Two. As far as your brain is concerned, you are giving it the message that weight gain is a huge threat to you and is something that should be feared.

A FEW KEY CONCEPTS OF IMPLICIT
BIAS AND FEAR OF WEIGHT GAIN

- Implicit biases are pervasive. The belief that thin is good and fat is bad is an implicit bias that is culturally held and therefore the vast majority of people in our culture have some level of unconscious fear of weight gain and/or fatphobia.

- Doctors, healthcare providers, scientific researchers, therapists, dieticians, and (especially) eating disorder professionals are not immune to fear of weight gain and fatphobia. Unfortunately, they are often the people who are most resistant to the idea that they have this implicit bias.

- When a person develops a restrictive eating disorder, they start acting very consistently as if weight gain is a threat to them. This avoidant behaviour further confirms to the brain that weight gain is, indeed, a threat, and increases fear of weight gain to a whole new level. This can result in a full-blown HPA-axis fight-or-flight response in the brain when doing anything that could potentially lead to weight gain such as eating more or moving less.

- Implicit bias and explicit bias around weight gain and fatphobia often exist together. So a person may have some awareness of their fatphobia, but not be fully aware of the extent to which it goes. They may be aware of some of their fatphobic or fear of weight gain thoughts, but unaware of the way that their beliefs shape their problem-solving, decision making, assumptions, day-to-day actions, reactions, and how it affects their nervous system responses.

- The implicit associations we hold do not necessarily align with our declared beliefs or even reflect stances we would explicitly or publically endorse. Hence, an eating-disorder therapist may outwardly declare that they are a HAES treatment provider, and still imply to a client that the client should restrict food when they have reached their "target" weight. Hence, a treatment provider who has not done their work around their own implicit bias against weight gain or larger bodies is a liability in the eating disorder treatment field.

The good news: our brains are incredible at learning and we are able to alter our implicit biases if we do the rewiring work required to change that belief system.

CHAPTER TWO - UNDERSTANDING FEAR

So, we've established that fear of weight gain exists. Now we need to work out what to do about it. First, we need to understand fear. This chapter will outline some key concepts about fear.

HOW FEAR WORKS IN THE BRAIN

(I'm going to keep this brief. If you need a longer and more in-depth explanation of fear, go find a neuroscientist. This is the two-cent tour of one aspect of fear research that I am interested in as I believe it is relevant to understanding how to rewire fear of weight gain.)

Some theorists say emotions like fear were inherited from our more primate ancestors and are therefore wired into our limbic system (caveperson brain), the fear-center being the amygdala.[1][2] [3] Brain studies show that the amygdala is activated when a threat is present. The amygdala detects a threat then activates the appropriate behavioural and physiological fear responses[4].

The idea that fear has unconscious and conscious elements is interesting to me, because I believe that the bulk of my own fear of weight gain was unconscious. The *"Defensive Survival Circuit View"* is one theory that describes subcortical circuits in the brain that are wired to respond to innate and learned threats once threats are detected. These circuits, if activated, indirectly contribute to the feeling of fear, but their activity alone doesn't constitute fear. This concept is put forward by Joseph LeDoux, and it serves to try and explain why species of animal that may be considered as unable to feel "emotions" as humans experience them, can and do react to threat. Hence the idea that, on a base-level, the brain detects and processes threats subconsciously, while the attribution of emotions happens in a separate part of the brain that humans have but some animals don't.

This idea of unconscious threat processing in humans has been tested by scientists doing things like flashing frightening images at people too fast for them to actually report that they have seen them (like the subliminal messaging images that conspiracy theorists love) and then measuring activation in the amygdala.[5] [6] What happens is the participants don't report feeling consciously afraid, but their amygdala activation indicates that a fear response occurred.

These theories on fear describe mechanisms that mean if you, for example, see a snake, there are two sets of circuits in your brain that process that information and contribute to your "feeling" (or not!) of fear.[7] On the most basic level, there are cortical circuits involving your visual cortex that is seeing and detecting the snake visually. Then, on a more higher-brain level, there are your memory systems that are remembering that snakes can be venomous, and your cognitive systems related to your general networks of cognition are all involved in your conscious experience of seeing the snake. At the same time, subcortical defensive survival circuits centered on the amygdala control your innate behavioral and physiological responses that are involved in threat detection. That's a very simplified version of a very complicated system because all I really want you to understand is that scientists believe that there are subcortical circuits in the brain that detect and process fear in a way that is not conscious to us.

So, with that in mind, could it be that upon seeing high calorie food, my amygdala was activated and processing a "threat" even though I wouldn't necessarily consciously feel the feeling of fear? I would say this was a possibility, based on the way I would behave. Because although I rarely detected what I would describe as "fear," I would act ... weird.

So, these "defensive survival circuits" in the limbic brain modulate the experience of fear, but are not directly responsible for the conscious experience itself. Cool. That means I reacted like a rabbit seeing a fox when I saw cake — I was outta there — but I didn't always consciously feel afraid of the cake. I just knew I wanted to leave the room.

This doesn't mean I would never experience fear directly. Say, for example, I saw a big birthday cake in the room, but I stayed. At some point — probably the point that someone had cut the cake and was handing me a slice — I would consciously detect something related to fear: I would feel hot and sweaty and stressed. So the defensive survival unit is like the really primitive, early warning, fear detection, while the conscious experience of fear may or may not be needed in order to get you to remove yourself from the situation.

All that, by the way, is theory. We don't have solid "facts" on anything when it comes to theories on fear and how all those systems work. There is still a lot of debate in the field of neuroscience as to what the definition of fear actually is, which is why I'm not going to wander too far into all of that, as interesting as it is. I'm not going to pretend I understand the complexities of it either. Nor, for the purposes of this book, do I think I need to. I just need to establish that it is likely that fear has both conscious and unconscious components and that these components would explain why some of us who consciously *want* to gain weight don't *act* as if we want to gain weight.

Fear is Healthy. Fear Protects

Fear is not an enemy — far from it!. Fear is extremely good for you. It's good for all of us. If early humans hadn't had a robust fear response, none of us would be here. Everyone would have been eaten by bears or sabertooth tigers and that would have been that. Fear stops you from doing dumb shit that could kill you.

Sometimes I think that we have a tendency, culturally, to down-talk many of the functions of our bodies and brains. We talk about menstrual cycles as if they are an inconvenience rather than a life-creating miracle. We talk about hunger as if it is a vice, rather than a life-sustaining biological system of great intelligence We talk about fear as if it is a weakness rather than a life-preserving warning system. My God, we humans can be so very condescending towards our bodies.

Just like your sex drive, your fear response exists for an incredibly good reason, so let us start this book with the understanding that we have to be respectful of fear. It saved your ancestors from all sorts of sticky ends. Fear is your guardian angel, and sometimes she gets a little over-protective, and sometimes she tries to keep you safe from things that actually were never going to hurt you, but even with all that in mind, she is still a guardian angel ... we want her and need her.

And another reminder: your body does everything for a reason, even when you can't work out what that reason is. Your body is never stupid. Just because you can't work out the reason you are having a fear response to something doesn't mean that there isn't one. It just means you didn't work it out yet.

So, if you have a working and functional fear response, be proud of it! The reason that most of us have very good fear responses is because we have had ancestors who had good fear responses. We know this, because they are the ones who survived long enough to have offspring. People with inadequate fear responses go on to win Darwin Awards. In its simplest form, fear is a danger warning in our brains. Nobody enjoys the sound of a fire alarm going off, but I imagine we can all agree that having a fire detection and warning system in the house is a good thing.

Early humans, like I said, had predators to deal with. If you think about it, there were probably lots of things seven million years ago, when humans started to evolve, that could kill you. Not just predators — other humans, the environment, the weather, ... famine. Plenty of things that the human brain needed to develop an aversion to, or a response to. For that reason, the fear center of the human brain was one of the first (well, technically second) parts to develop. In short, according to a bloke called MacLean who developed something called the *Triune Brain* model, the reptilian or primal brain is in control of automatic and built-in self-preserving behavioural tendencies — the things we do that stop us from walking off cliffs like lemmings. Just because your reptile brain developed yonks ago doesn't mean it is irrelevant now. No, unlike your 2005 Super Nintendo, your brainstem area is still very relevant. It still keeps you safe. Sure, you may not stumble across a bear in your day-to-day existence, but there are still plenty of threats out there.

The rest of our brain — the parts that make us smart and logical and able to talk and do math and post funny memes on the internet — all developed later. The parts of the brain that deal with survival came first, and they are rather like the foundations of a house in that they are harder to get at if you want to remodel or restructure them, and you are not always dealing with things you can see.

FEAR SPARKS A SYMPATHETIC NERVOUS SYSTEM RESPONSE

Your autonomic nervous system has two gears - parasympathetic (rest and digest) and sympathetic (fight or flight). When everything is well, we cruise along in our parasympathetic nervous system (PNS). Think of this one as the "normal" nervous system. This is you doing your thing, all calm and relaxed. The sympathetic nervous system, on the other hand, is the emergency gear. Think the fire alarm going off, people jumping out of burning buildings, that sort of thing.

The fear response has the effect of switching you from your chilled-out PNS to your holy-crap-here-we-go SNS. When your brain perceives a threat, (for me, that would have been my mother looming over me with a slice of cake) your adrenal glands secrete adrenaline. This adrenaline causes blood to flow away from your brain's frontal lobe (that is the part of your brain that thinks rationally) and redirects it towards the deeper, survival-orientated caveperson parts of your brain such as the amygdala. Your SNS is like the top gear in your car in that when you are in it, everything is running at a higher rate than it really is meant to. Your heart is pounding. Your breathing is fast. You may feel hot. Your blood pressure rises and your muscles tense. Jeez, being in your SNS is tiring! And anxiety is a form of fear. Anxiety is generally the more long-term, sustained version of our fear response. But anxiety is exhausting too, because you are still operating in a higher gear.

When we are in emergency gear we don't always make good decisions because we make fast decisions. Nobody can be continually driving around like a bank-robber on the run and be doing well in terms of smart choices. Unfortunately, this is exactly what most of us are doing when we have an eating disorder because we are constantly being pushed into our sympathetic nervous system by our fear of weight gain.

Once you are in your SNS it can be quite difficult to get back into your PNS. The reason for that is because your brain's fear response doesn't want you to go back to chillout mode before it is very sure the threat has passed. When the threat is weight gain, it is always imminent, and hence the long-term anxiety and state of stress that many people with eating disorders live in.

The good news is that if we rewire fear of weight gain and teach the brain that weight gain is not a threat, it will no longer have to keep you cycling into your SNS whenever someone offers you with a cookie. And I can't tell you what a relief it is to not get thrown into an internal panic whenever food is present. This — not being on a constant SNS ride — is what recovery really is.

FEAR IS SUSPICIOUS

Fear is like that annoying person who tells you *"I'll believe it when I see it."* Fear doesn't take your word for it. Fear has to be shown things IRL to convince it to change its mind. That, by the way, is also functional. Say, for example, if fear was easily swayed, and all you had to do was tell it *"snakes won't hurt you"* and it would believe you ... well, our ancestors would have all died of snake bites.

Oh no. You tell fear *"snakes won't hurt you,"* and it responds with *"You shut your mouth, I don't believe any of your shit."* Fear demands to be *shown* that snakes won't hurt you. Fear will only change its mind about snakes if you physically walk up to and touch the snake over and over again. Fear wants to see you touch the snake 200 times before it is convinced the snake is safe. Sure, that's inconvenient. Sure it takes time and effort. But do you know what is even more inconvenient: being killed by a snake bite, that's what.

It is by design that fear is hard to shake once it is established. That is another very important and desirable function of fear. It is also one I want you to remember as you read this book: you can't convince your brain not to be afraid of something by asking or telling it. You have to *show* it, over and over again.

Talk is cheap and words don't prove shit as far as your brain is concerned. The proof is in the doing.

FEAR IS FUELED BY AVOIDANCE

Avoiding something you are afraid of has the short term effect of making you feel safe, and the long term consequence of making you more fearful. In my experience, the act of avoidance itself can cause a person to fear the thing that they are avoiding if the avoidant behaviour is persistent enough.

I remember when I was a pony-mad kid I once saw a huge spider in my favourite pony Casper's stall at the riding stable. Obviously, because spiders are awful, I started to avoid going into Casper's stall. This made me sad because I wanted to go and see Casper but I wouldn't because I was afraid there might be a spider in there. The longer I avoided that stall, the more fearful I became. Additionally, I remember beginning to become afraid of not only going into Casper's stall, but of going into any of the stalls. My logic being that if there was a spider in Casper's stall, there were likely spiders in the other stalls too. My fear spread.

Avoidance makes fear grow. I guess that's why the saying goes that you should get back on the horse after a fall. (I personally always used to get back on the horse after a fall until I went to the doctor with a concussion and she was utterly horrified when I told her I got back on after hitting my head. She told me that's ridiculously dangerous because apparently a second knock to the head can be deadly if you have a concussion. She made me vow never to get back on a horse after hitting my head. So maybe don't take *"get back on the horse"* literally.) Anyway, at some point I must have got myself together and got over my fear of spiders in horse's stalls, because avoiding going into horse's stalls becomes a major obstacle when you are an aspiring equestrian. I have to admit, spiders still evoke a fear reaction in me. I could rewire it, but I'm not going to because I'm able to live a happy and fulfilling life by simply avoiding the little bastards.

Now, think about how avoidant we become when we develop a restrictive eating disorder. Avoidant of anything that could potentially lead to weight gain. Avoidant of people who might make us eat. Avoidant of situations involving food. Avoidant of high-calorie food. Avoidant of high-fat food. Avoidant of rest. Some of us spend years and years acting in a way that is highly avoidant of weight gain, and this massively increases our fear of weight gain. Our brains are watching us act in a way that is avoidant of anything that may lead to weight gain and concluding that weight gain must be a threat.

Persistent avoidance also makes fear move from specific to general. If a person gets bitten by a dog they may start by avoiding the specific dog that bit them, but this fear of being bitten may lead to them avoiding all dogs. And the more they avoid dogs, the greater their fear of being bitten by a dog becomes. We see this a lot in eating disorders also. One might begin to avoid certain dairy products because they are considered high in fat, but this avoidance spreads over time to include all dairy products. Most of us have experienced that if we begin to avoid a certain type of food, our reluctance to eat other types of foods grows.

Avoidance-created fear is a big problem with orthorexia, as people begin to avoid certain brands, ingredients, labels, additives, etc., etc. The more types of food you avoid, the more anxiety you feel over new and unknown foods, and the more inclined you are to eat the same narrow food set day in and day out. So you do just that, and the longer you spend eating the same foods every day the harder it is to venture into eating something different. I know this one only too well. Groundhog Day when it came to food. I was so very bored with eating the same foods and yet so very not up for changing anything.

Orthorexia is marked by anxiety around eating foods considered "unhealthy," and what tends to happen is this list of "unhealthy" foods grows and grows. Orthorexia is another thing that has a basis in our cultural beliefs (low-fat food are good and high fat foods are bad; apples are good and crisps are bad; kale is good and bread is bad etc.) which make it difficult to overcome because our brains continuously justify the restriction and have lots of backup from the "health" community that congratulates the restriction of "unhealthy" foods. Whenever there is a cultural judgement placed on food, it is much more difficult to rewire your fear of that food. It's like trying to overcome your fear of snakes while everyone around is shouting *"don't touch the snake it will kill you!"* (And this is exactly one of the reasons I have such a problem with food judgements being present in eating disorder treatment.)

Orthorexia is a detriment to health, both physical and mental, and orthorexia fears need to be rewired just like fear of weight gain fears do if a person wants to fully recover. You cannot have full mental freedom when you are still eating to a set of food rules. If you are afraid and avoidant of "unhealthy" foods, you will continue to have food-related anxiety. Having any degree of food-related anxiety is not freedom from an eating disorder, and therefore my definition of full recovery includes no orthorexia or fear of "unhealthy" foods. You can absolutely achieve this if you do the rewiring work. And, you guessed it, that rewiring work entails you eating all of the foods that you are afraid of or feel resistance to or consider "unhealthy" until you no longer feel anxiety and/or judgement around eating those foods. *That* is true freedom.

FEAR IS EMOTIONAL

Emotion is to fear what muscles are to movement. And before you get all condescending and judgey about what it means to be emotional, let me tell you that emotions are the epitome of function as far as your brain is concerned. Emotion is the tool that your brain uses to influence you to do things. Emotion is the catalyst for many of our behaviours and actions. And according to people who debate things such as the meaning of life, it is the presence of an emotional response that defines what it is to be conscious. [8]

Emotions incite us to behave in certain ways. If our brain wants us to do something, it uses emotion to make us feel like we *want* to do that thing. If our brain doesn't want us to do something, it uses emotion to make us feel like we *don't want* to do that thing. For example, if someone is nice to you, your brain uses a variety of emotions that are warm and fuzzy to make you feel like you want to hang out with that person. That's because, as far as your caveperson brain is concerned, your chances of survival are higher if you stay close to people who are nice to you. They might give you stuff. They might protect you. You guys should, therefore, hang out.

If someone is mean to you, your brain uses emotion to make you feel like you want to stay away from that person. That's because your chances of survival are jeopardized by other humans who don't like you — especially if resources are scarce. That's why it is normal not to want to hang out with people who are arseholes. If your brain wants you to reproduce, it uses emotion to make you feel horny. That's because reproduction is desirable for gene survival. If your brain wants you to look after your offspring, it uses emotion to make you feel bonded to them. That's because having a parent invested in the survival of their offspring is also desirable for gene survival. Emotion is always functional, and you can usually trace its function back to the Selfish Gene theory.

It behoves your genes to keep you alive. Hence, if your brain has established that something is a threat to you, your brain will use emotion to keep you away from that thing. Luckily for me, you don't need to be particularly clever to see how that makes sense. If you have a fear of snakes and a snake slithers into the room, your brain's job is to keep you the hell away from that murdering death-serpent. The fear-response-center of your brain will swiftly provide you with a hefty serving of the fear emotion and, in doing so, will influence you to physically move your body away from the snake. In this instance, the emotion of fear caused you to move your feet, and as a result, you are safely away from that snake. A lot of the time this all happens so fast that the higher-up part of your brain doesn't even have a chance to get involved. Bravo brain, you kept the human away from the threat. Job done.

And here is where we get to the part of explaining all those negative emotions that are so very prevalent with eating disorders; namely: guilt, shame, disgust, anxiety, and regret. These are the emotions best suited to the situation of warning you away from anything that may lead to weight gain. Your brain fears weight gain. Your brain's job is to protect you from weight gain. Your brain uses emotion to influence your behaviours. You eat more food than usual — an action your brain perceives may lead to weight gain. *"Oh no,"* thinks your brain, *"my human has done something that could lead to weight gain, I have to save them! I know, I will use guilt emotions to make them feel like they don't want to do that again ..."* So ... your brain uses the emotions of guilt, shame, disgust, and regret to make you feel like you don't want to do the action of eating more than usual again in the future. And it works. So. Very. Well.

All these negative emotions that most of us are inundated with when we have an eating disorder aren't just your brain being mean for kicks and giggles. It's not your brain just throwing around shitty feelings for the heck of it. They are your brain "protecting" you from something your brain perceives as a threat (weight gain.) These negative emotions are not dysfunction. Far from it. They are actually a wonderfully well functioning fear response at work. Don't get me wrong, it's a bitch, but it's a well-meaning and functional bitch.

FEAR DOESN'T HESITATE

Response times are somewhat critical when it comes to fear. In order to keep you safe, the brain has to be able to react to any threat immediately. It doesn't have time to dawdle. It can't pause to check in with your executive brain and ask permission. The fear-response-center of your brain is a little like the emergency fire department. If there is a fire they don't wait for permission to go and put it out, they ring that bell and twizzle down the fire-person's pole as fast as they can. In fact, any delay caused by waiting to get the go-ahead could result in tragedy. The fire crew is designed to react fast and autonomously to threat. So is your amygdala (that's the fear-response center). If your amygdala had to run upstairs and get permission from your executive brain whenever it needed to keep you safe from imminent threat ... well, we would probably be extinct. The bear certainly wouldn't be waiting for permission to eat you.

The instant nature of fear emotions is the main thing that makes them so bloody difficult to deal with when we need to rewire that fear. There just isn't a ton of thinking space. Note that I said *difficult*, which is far from *impossible*. It is like any situation where you know that there is not a lot of time once things actually kick off, you just have to be very organised ahead of kick-off. You have to anticipate what your response is going to be, and set yourself up to jump in and change it. Anyway, we will get into how to overcome these ever-so-strong-and-convincing fear emotions in a couple of chapters.

FEAR OFTEN DISGUISES

Another thing to keep in mind: not all fear emotions dress themselves up as straightforward fear. Your brain will use whichever emotion is most relevant to the situation. If you have a fear of public speaking, anxiety is the most common tactic your brain will use to keep you away from that threat. If your brain wants to keep you away from maggots, disgust would be the relevant emotion. If you act against a person your brain considers to be a friend in a way that could cause them to dislike you, guilt is the way your brain reminds you that being alone has a lower rate of survival for cave-people. The emotions of anxiety, guilt, disgust, shame, and regret can all be used when our brains want to steer us away from something it perceives to be a threat.

We will discuss some common ways that fear presents itself with eating disorders in Chapter Three.

FEAR IS PREDICTABLE

For me, predicting my emotional responses was one of the most effective ways for me to not get caught up in them. If I called my fear response before it happened, I would be able to sit back and observe my own emotional state better, and this placed me in the seat of the observer rather than in the seat of the reactor.

I think the reason this worked so well for me is because I really like being right. I'd say to myself *"I bet that after eating this cake I will feel the guilt emotion,"* then I would eat the cake and sit back and watch for that guilt to come, Then, when the guilt came, I would think *"see, I knew it!"* and feel all smug about calling it right, rather than actually feeling guilty. When one is feeling smug, one is not panicking or freaking out. For me, predicting emotion was what allowed me to not get caught up in the emotion when it came.

What is actually going on when we predict our emotional response, is that we are preparing ourselves for it, and in doing so, we are better at staying in our parasympathetic nervous system and not getting all caught up in the emotional response and therefore in our sympathetic nervous system. If you are in your parasympathetic nervous system, you can make more logical and rational choices, and you can better choose not to allow your emotions to take you on a rollercoaster ride.

In recovery, you need to use the predictability of your fear response to help you overcome your fear. If you are expecting it, you can be prepared for it. I find that one of the reasons people don't do this in recovery is because they don't understand that they have fear of weight gain, and/or they don't understand that recovery is about rewiring this fear. I find that once people with eating disorders understand that the negative emotions they experience are a fear response, they are actually very good at managing them and thus overcoming fear of weight gain.

Say, for example, you have a fear of snakes and you decide you want to overcome that fear. If you volunteer to go and touch a snake, you are expecting to feel afraid — terrified — when you go and do that. That expectation allows you to prep yourself. You will take a good amount of time to psych yourself up and it is doing this that allows you to be successful in touching the snake. The fact that you feel afraid when you go to touch the snake is no surprise to you. You are ready for it. Being ready for it means that you can push through it and touch the snake just like you had psyched yourself up to do.

We should be doing the same thing in eating disorder recovery — prepping ourselves for the abundance of guilt, shame, disgust, and regret we are going to feel after doing something that our brains are afraid of, such as: eating more, eating differently, not exercising, not purging, etc., etc.

But a lot of people don't because the overcoming fear aspect of recovery isn't given the importance it deserves. If you don't prepare for the feelings of guilt, shame, disgust and fear, you will be sucked into them, over and over again. And that's just tiring. Emotions are exhausting! It's no wonder so many people get burnt out by recovery when they are spending all their time being in that heightened emotional state. It's tiring just to think about it, let alone do it. It is so much easier to take the seat of the observer — which is a much calmer, less exhausting place to be, because it is your parasympathetic nervous system — if we are anticipating the emotions.

And here is where you have a head start already, because if there is one thing that is true about eating disorder emotional responses it is that they are very predictable. I can tell you right now that if you go and eat a donut you will experience the feeling of guilt afterwards. Am I a mind reader? Nope. It's just that bloody predictable. Honestly, eating disorders are a gift in that sense.

You *know* that your brain will generate negative emotions when you do something that could potentially lead to weight gain. It's probably already happened a hundred times in the past week. Your fear response is very reliable like that. The reason your brain is doing this is because it has a fear of weight gain. So now you need to prepare for those emotions and then, rather than try and avoid them, provoke them. Because it is only by doing the things that we are afraid of that we can show our brains we don't need to be afraid of those things. Avoiding your fears only amplifies them.

The belief systems and "behavioural reinforcers" cycle of doom

When you have a fear-based belief system, avoidant behaviours develop and become established. If you are afraid of flying, you avoid vacations that involve leaving the ground. If you are afraid of spiders, you avoid basements and sinks. If you are afraid of weight gain, you develop a whole battery of weird and avoidant behaviours, many of which I outlined in detail in *Rehabilitate, Rewire, Recover!* We are talking things like food rules, compulsive movement, purging and other compensatory behaviours, fear foods, rigid routines, etc., etc.

Now, initially, you developed these tendencies to help you avoid the thing that you were afraid of. However, over time, these behaviours serve to reinforce your fear. And thus we have the cycle of doom. You started not eating pizza because you feared potential weight gain, but now your avoidance of pizza reinforces your fear of weight gain. You started exercise because you feared weight gain, but now your continued exercise reinforces your fear of weight gain. You started purging because you feared weight gain, but the act of purging also reinforces fear of weight gain. Behaviours that developed as a means to help you avoid the thing you are afraid of go on to reinforce the fear on a daily basis.

This is because the act of avoidance reinforces fear. Your brain is watching you avoid all these foods that could potentially lead to weight gain and concluding that weight gain must be a threat — why would you be avoiding it so consistently if it wasn't? It is also because behaviours that you developed to help you avoid weight gain are directly linked to fear of weight gain. You can't teach your brain that a fear is not relevant while you are still actively engaging in behaviors that are linked to it.

It is super-duper important that you understand this cycle and break it. You cannot rewire a fear that you are actively reinforcing. It just will not work. You can be eating all the donuts in the world and your fear of weight gain will remain if you are still engaging in compulsive exercise and food rules that serve to reinforce fear of weight gain.

CHAPTER THREE - WHY REWIRING FEAR OF WEIGHT GAIN IS ESSENTIAL FOR FULL RECOVERY

What we are dealing with in eating disorders and fear of weight gain is a very functional fear response. Hence, if you ask me, eating disorder recovery is about fear response management. The good news is that when we understand that eating disorder recovery is largely about overcoming a fear response, recovery is no longer this cloudy mystery concept paved with feel-good memes, cheesy quotes pasted on images of rainbows, and pictures of laughing girls dressed in comfy robes sitting with kittens touting messages of "self-care." (For the record I have nothing against sitting in comfy robes with kittens. I would pay good money to do this, it's just not going to get you recovered from an eating disorder. Which is really a great shame.)

When you see recovery as fear-response management, it becomes real and the path becomes clear. You know what it looks like because you have done fear-response management before, and often. Whenever you have done something that has scared you, you have managed your fear response. Every time you do something that makes your heart beat so loud you think everyone else can hear it, you are working through your sympathetic nervous system response to something that feels threatening. Luckily for me, as I kid I was scared of many things, including the dark, so I got to practice fear-response management a lot.

For at least a year after watching *Jaws* when I was about eight, I jumped in and out of bed because I was convinced that Jaws, the Great White Shark, was under my bed. Finally, at the wise age of nine, I decided that I was too old to have a fear like this. I forced myself to walk right up to my bed and slowly get into it. Every time I approached the gap between the edge of the bed and the floor with my feet, I would feel panicky energy moving from my toes to my knees. I would want so very badly to jump. But I made myself linger there with my toes dangerously close to that dark abyss of the bed-floor gap. Oh, the relief when I lifted my feet up into the safety of the top of my bed. I'd make myself lift them up slowly and resist the urge to rush that last part despite the image in my head I had of Jaws lurching up from under the bed and eating me alive. I was determined not to give in to the fear.

As stupid and childish as that sounds, the experience of working though my Jaws-under-the-bed fears as a kid was wonderful practice for managing my nervous system while overcoming fear. That feeling of forcing myself to act calmly while I'm panicking is familiar and practiced to me. Sometimes I wonder if this is why children's imaginations run wild and make them afraid of very irrational things, such as a 20ft shark living under a 6ft landlocked bed. Maybe these ridiculous fears exist because we need to practice getting to know our fear responses so we can have some degree of ability to manage them in later life.

Regardless, the main point is that you *do* know how to overcome fear. Whether it is fear of sharks under beds, or spiders in stables, or having to stand up and answer a question in class, you *do* know how to do things that scare you. You have reference points for when you have done this in the past. This is not unknown territory for you. Nor is it anything particularly complicated or magical. In many cases it *is* actually as simple as repeatedly doing what you are afraid of until you are no longer afraid of it. Sure, overcoming fear is not particularly easy. It takes effort, but you can't really say you don't know *how* to do it.

But it's difficult. Why do I have to?

Because you can't fully recover when you still have fear of weight gain.

Fear of weight gain is responsible for the negative emotions that are generated when you do anything that could lead to weight gain (such as eat more food than usual), or if you don't do something that aids in the suppression of your body weight (such as *not* exercise, or *not* purge). Fear of weight gain is also responsible for the negative emotions that your brain generates about your body when you gain weight.

You can test this out by doing something that provokes your fear of weight gain fear response. Try eating more food than usual; or don't exercise; or eat a higher calorie version of something; or don't purge. Then watch as your brain uses the emotions of guilt, shame, disgust, and regret to attempt to convince you not to do that again. The more afraid your brain is of weight gain, the stronger these emotions will feel. Also, when you do this, notice that by anticipating and watching out for these emotions, you are more able to stay out of the drama. This is because you have placed yourself in the "seat of the observer" when it comes to your brain's functioning, and once you are in that seat, you are more able to not get caught up in the emotion. This, by the way, is mindfulness. It's what meditation and all that is supposed to teach us: to be able to step out of and observe our emotional responses rather than be *in* our emotional responses. The reason it works is because, when you step back from the emotions generated by your fear response, you move from your sympathetic nervous system into your parasympathetic nervous system and thus access the parts of your brain that help you think more rationally.

A QUICK INTERJECTION ON
NEGATIVE BODY IMAGE

Negative body image is a product of fear of weight gain. It's the same mechanism we have already discussed in terms of your fear response generating negative emotions:.

1. Your brain has been taught that weight gain is a threat to you. When your brain believes that something is a threat to you it is your brain's job to keep you away from this thing. The tool that the brain uses to influence your actions is emotion.
2. You gain weight. Your brain sees that you have gained weight. Your brain believes it must protect you from weight gain, so your fear-response to weight gain is activated.
3. Your fear-response "protects" you from weight gain by generating negative emotions about your weight gain and your body in a bid to influence you to want to lose weight.
4. You feel like shit and want to lose weight.

The most appropriate emotions to deliver to you that will assist in this task are feelings of disgust and rejection around your higher-weight body. It works really well. Negative body image emotions feel horrid and most people can't put up with it for long before they want to comply with what the fear of weight gain is asking for and lose weight.

Okay, back to why you have to do the rewiring ....

Now, should you try and recover without rewiring fear of weight gain ... all those negative emotions are going to persist. People do this when they gain weight but don't do the rewiring. This results in a higher bodyweight and a pretty much constant and very loud negative body image tirade. Nobody can sustain sitting in a bath of consistent negative thoughts about their body indefinitely. Most people last up to three months before they throw in the towel, declare that they can't do recovery, and return to restricting, or purging, or exercising.

Rewiring fear of weight gain makes recovery sustainable because when your brain no longer sees weight gain as a threat, it no longer needs to generate negative emotions designed to keep you away from weight gain. Nor does it need to generate negative emotions about your body designed to cause you to want to lose weight again. Therefore, it is no longer a fight. It is no longer difficult to maintain your recovered, unsuppressed body, because your negative body image is vastly reduced.

TL;DR: Negative body image is a product of fear of weight gain and, therefore, negative body image emotions will continue to be generated until fear of weight gain is rewired.

WHAT FEAR OF WEIGHT GAIN LOOKS LIKE

Those of you who read my blog will recognise this chapter. It was writing a blog on what different expressions of fear look like that lead to the idea of writing this book on fear of weight gain. Don't worry I haven't totally short-changed you as I have elaborated on the original blog post.

The confusing thing about fear of weight gain is that it doesn't always *look* like fear. It's not like someone pulls out a slice of pizza and you throw your hands in the air and run away screaming with your hair standing on end. Nope, fear often looks like resistance, excuses, squirming, discomfort, an overactive brain, a tendency not to want to walk into unfamiliar situations, a tendency to isolate, and wanting to stick to the things that you know you feel safe with. Fear is often very subtle. Well, I guess that depends on the situation, as I was also known to be very explosive, as my go-to fear response was frequently anger.

It took me about 10 years to realise that my tendency to hit the roof in rage whenever my mother offered me food was actually an expression of fear. I'm kind of embarrassed it took me that long as this behaviour of mine was so incredibly abnormal, yet in the moment it felt warranted (to me at least). It seems so obvious now that someone popping their head around the door and asking *"Darling, would you like a sandwich?"* should not provoke murderous thoughts and a tirade of insults. It dawned on me at some point that it was actually my anger that was inappropriate, not my mother. Who would have thought?

Once I recognised that my anger-response to being offered food was off kilter, I was able to join the dots. *Why do I split my wig when offered food? Because being offered food feels like a threat. Why does someone offering me food feel like such a threat? Because I am afraid of weight gain? But I want to gain weight. I hate being thin. Then why do I still restrict food and compulsively exercise? Why aren't I acting as if I want to gain weight? Maybe there is a part of me that doesn't? Maybe I do fear weight gain after all?*

Fear of weight gain was a hard pill for me to swallow because, consciously, I didn't fear weight gain. Consciously, I *wanted* to gain weight. But, as I have explained in the previous chapters, fear is not always conscious, and despite wanting to gain weight I could also see that my actions and behaviours were *avoidant* of weight gain. My reactions were certainly indicative that some part of my brain viewed weight gain as a threat. Understanding that my anger was also a symptom of fear was helpful to me. Not least because it piqued my interest. I became curious about my absurd reactions, and that curiosity resulted in me exploring them. I would feel my brain move into a rage after being offered food, and a part of me would step back from that rage and think, "*Well, isn't that interesting that an offer of a digestive biscuit can make me feel like burning the house down?*" As soon as you become curious about and start watching your emotions like that, you step outside of them a little bit, and in doing so, you take one foot out of your sympathetic nervous system and place it into your parasympathetic nervous system. And that is where you begin to have an ounce of control and rationality.

As I explored my fear, I began to understand that anger was one of a variety of fear-responses that I frequently exhibited and that a lot of the "weird shit" I did was actually an adaptation of a fear response. My fear-response of choice would depend on what felt the most suitable in any given situation. It wouldn't do, for example, to get snark with every person who offered me food in the way I did with my mother. No, I saved the megabitch version of me for the people who loved me most. Those lucky souls. People I knew less well would get the more socially acceptable flight, freeze, or fawn.

FIGHT, FLIGHT, FREEZE, FAWN

The Four-Fs are sympathetic nervous system fear responses. I had my go-tos, but they were also situation dependent. If you recognise yourself doing any of these, then you are probably dealing with a fear-response to eating food (which is really a fear of weight gain.)

FIGHT

Looks like this:

"Darling, would you like a slice of cake?"

"Fuck you I won't do what you tell me! How dare you ask me that! You're the most horrible person alive. Oh, and by the way everybody knows that cake is bad for you and will kill you. So you're basically trying to make me eat something that will kill me and that is pure evil and you should be ashamed of yourself. Don't come near me with that artificial-ingredient-laden cake of death! I hate you."

Also looks like this (aggressive justification):

"Did you know that obesity is on the rise and according to a study done in yadda yadda yadda cake is one of the leading causes of obesity? With all the research that shows us that saturated fat is one of the leading causes of high cholesterol and heart disease, it would be irresponsible of me to eat cake because I want to look after my body. My decision not to eat cake is 100 percent to do with me being health conscious and well informed."

The "fight" response looks like aggression, but aggression in this day and age can also look like being a literature-spewing know-it-all. I was prone to the former, but I would also use the latter to make my over-the-top reaction seem justified. So I would bite my mum's head off then back it up by spurting out some recent study on the health benefits of starving oneself.

I've heard plenty of stories of kids with eating disorders throwing plates of food across the room, and even getting physical with their parents in order to avoid eating. Anger is most commonly used towards people we are close enough to to be able to get away with it. So for me, my mother got the brunt of my anger fear-response. I would see red when she offered me food. I would feel so angry I would get dizzy. Livid. And I would be vile. Then, after my mother (the threat) removed herself from my presence, I would usually calm down and feel just horrid. The, I'd feel guilty for being so terrible to her. That's a pretty standard sympathetic to parasympathetic nervous system switch at work. Whilst in the sympathetic nervous system (fight or flight, etc.) the anger felt warranted. When calmed down and in the parasympathetic nervous system (rest and digest) I could see my anger was an over-reaction and I felt crap about it.

Despite the fact it turned me into a real bitch, I'm thankful for my fight response because, in the long-run, it was the pure aggressive nature of my reaction to being offered food that started me on the path to recognising how fucked up I was. That's the only way one can really describe a person who screams at someone else for offering them a biscuit: fucked up. Had my fear-response not been as bloody audacious, I might not have ever clocked on to it. So yeah, thanks Mum.

FLIGHT

Looks like this:

"Would you like a slice of cake?"

"Er, yeah, sure but, I just realised I have to go and do that thing with that person that I said I was going to do. Sorry. Got to run. Bye"

Also looks like this (avoidance):

"Would you come to my birthday party?"

"I'm sorry I'm busy that night"

"But I didn't tell you when it is yet ..."

The flight response is basically running away. Alright, it might not look like actually turning tail and sprinting off, as that would be socially too weird, so it more commonly looks like very polite but obviously bollocks excuses. I would use this fear response when I was around people I didn't know so well: acquaintances, parents of friends, work colleagues, etc. I would find a reason to leave when feeling threatened with food. This would often happen at social gatherings. I'd get there, realise the threat of food was imminent, and apologetically excuse myself. Often the best excuse being *"I don't feel very well,"* or *"I have a headache."* Sometimes, I just wouldn't show up. I missed so many birthday parties, weddings, and celebrations when I had an eating disorder simply because I was avoiding food.

If I was at a party or gathering, the flight response, for me, would come into play in situations where the social trade-off of leaving felt low. Flight was more commonly my default response to social situations that I hadn't placed great importance on being at — drinks parties where nobody would really notice if I had left, etc. If, for whatever reason I felt social pressure to stay, I would be more likely to use the fawn response (outlined below).

FREEZE

Looks like this:

"Would you like a slice of cake?"

".... urm ...... I .... arg."

Also looks like this:

"Why haven't you stopped exercising?"

".... urm ...... I .... arg."

And this*:*

"What do you want for dinner?"

".... urm ...... I .... arg."

Brain freeze. Feelings of overwhelm. Often happens when having to make decisions about what to eat or in supermarkets trying to decide what to buy. For me, this looked like walking into a grocery shop and walking out an hour later having bought nothing. I would feel as if my brain had short-circuited. I felt utterly unable to make a decision over something as simple as what brand of tea to buy. This is often the reason people with eating disorders opt to eat the same foods day in and day out: because food-related decisions cause a sympathetic nervous system response when you have a fear of weight gain. Restaurant menus commonly elicit the freeze response. For many of us, this sort of silent head explosion is uncomfortable enough to make us avoid any situation where we might publically be surprised with food or have to make an on-the-spot food choice.

In a social situation, this would most often look like me totally ignoring the question or pretending I had not heard it.

The freeze response is also, I believe, one of the reasons that so many of us struggle to change our behaviours when we have an eating disorder. Every day I told myself I was going to eat more. Every evening I told myself that tomorrow I would give up exercise. Yet every day I ate in the same restrictive way. Every day I woke up, pulled on my trainers, and went for a run. I was frozen into my daily routine. This was frustrating to me and to everyone else. To the onlooker, it looks like you are not trying at all. It looks like nothing is happening. Trying to change — by eating more or exercising less — led to my fear-response kicking off, and my fear reaction a lot of the time was to freeze and therefore change nothing.

The freeze response makes one look and feel like an idiot. Ironically, it is the freeze response that most often leads therapists and dietitians to believe that the best course of action for a person with a restrictive eating disorder is to put them on a meal plan. Because that is easier and they don't have to think about or make food decisions. A lot of people with eating disorders think this is the solution too... Until they realise that it isn't. The reason that it doesn't help is because you don't rewire a fear response by avoiding the thing that you are afraid of. If you take someone who goes into freeze when having to make a food choice and put them on a meal plan, you are not fixing anything. You are just removing that particular source of fear and, in doing so, removing their ability to practice overcoming it on any level at all. Doing this can be a short-term plan for sure, but all too often it isn't used as a short-term solution. Rather, people are on meal plans for years and then they become so unpracticed at making food decisions they are rendered completely unconfident and reduced to a blithering, blubbering, wreck should their usual brand of breakfast cereal be unavailable.

Yes, the freeze response, like all fear responses, feels horrid. Yes, you still have to work though it and challenge it in order to rewire it. We will get to exactly how to do that in the next chapter

FAWN (AKA THE APPEASE RESPONSE)

Looks like this:

"Would you like a slice of cake?"

"Oh, yes, delicious, thank you, yum yum." (Takes the cake then pretends to eat it while carefully breaking it into crumbs between fingers and dropping it onto the rug under the table and praying the dog eats it before anyone notices.)

Also looks like this (compensating):

"Would you like to come out for pizza tonight?"

"Yes, I would absolutely love that!" (Then spends the entire day heavily restricting and exercising in preparation.)

I would do "fawn" in situations where I didn't feel I could get out of eating or I didn't feel that I could get away with leaving — smaller gatherings where it would look really off if I just got up and left.

If the social pressure to eat was too great or if it would draw a lot of attention or make me stand out if I refused something, I would act very pleased to take the food then make myself as small as possible, withdraw from the conversation, and focus my energy on trying to make it look like I was complying socially by eating the food whilst somehow getting rid of it. I would often pretend to eat — fake movements of my mouth, noises of appreciation, exclaiming afterwards how yummy it had been, etc., etc.

I'm sure people noticed me doing this but ignored it because it is awkward to ask someone *"Hey, why did you pretend to eat that honey-glazed cocktail sausage when you were actually shoving it into your coat pocket?"* It is not only weird to get caught doing this, it also looks kind of rude. It is a form of deceit — you are pretending to eat — that catches other people off-guard because they don't understand why you would do that. I did get caught a few times and it was very embarrassing because there is no suitable excuse to make for purposefully dropping food on another person's carpet or down the back of their sofa. (I'd like to take this moment to apologize to all the people who found mouldy food down the back of their sofas after having me round. Awful behaviour.).

I see compensating as a fawn response. We want to look normal, so we agree to going and doing things and eating things, but behind the scenes we are scrambling to make it "okay." So I would accept an invitation to go out for food, but I would spend the entire day beforehand eating only celery sticks. Purging can also be used as a form of compensation.

Basically, with the fawn response, we are faking it. Faking eating. Faking not being freaked out. Faking being happy. And most of the time we are doing this because it is upsetting to other people to see us not eat, so it is easier to pretend to go along with it.

ALL OF THE F'S ARE FUCKED UP

Fear responses such as the examples above are indicative that you have entered your sympathetic nervous system. We only enter our sympathetic nervous system when our brain detects a threat. If you are doing any of the above behaviours (or something similar), your brain sees food/weight gain as a threat. Entering your sympathetic nervous system when being presented with food is not a "normal" response and indicates a fear-based belief system (the belief that weight gain is a threat) that needs to be neurally rewired.

The examples I have written here to demonstrate different fight, flight, freeze and fawn responses are just a few examples of how fear responses can look when a person has an eating disorder. Everyone has responses that look different, but can probably be traced back to one of the Four-Fs. It doesn't matter which "F" you use, it's still fear and it is still fucked up because food should not elicit a fear response.

Overall, having a fear of weight gain is miserable. While you are having a fear response, you're not having any fun. If you are at a birthday party and all you can think about is how you are going to get away with not eating cake, you are not concentrating on enjoyment. Fear is very distracting in that sense.

I think it is worth remembering that fear can be unconscious also, and hence for many of us, we may have a fear reaction and not clock it as a fear reaction. That would happen a lot to me. I would be at a birthday party and feel twitchy and irritable and want to leave when the cake came out without having any conscious thought linking my discomfort to the cake. This happened a lot with my "fight" responses. I would be aggressive in my stance of not wanting to eat, but I wouldn't necessarily detect the fear that was present in myself—ironically, other people would often recognise fear in my responses before I would. For these reasons, some of us have to watch our own behaviours and work backwards from them to link them to fear. Regardless of how you do it, getting to know how fear presents itself in your behaviours is an important part of being able to rewire that fear.

FULL RECOVERY MEANS REWIRING FEAR

Fear *is* rewirable. You can teach your brain not to fear. Every person in recovery from an eating disorder needs to be given the message that they can do this.

Models of recovery that are actually just different ways of making your fear response tolerable are, in my opinion, not recovery. I have seen suggestions such as *"If you are afraid of going and eating restaurant food, just take your own food with you to the restaurant so that you don't have to deal with that fear."* When I read or hear of such things I just feel so sad. Telling someone to sidestep and/ or avoid their fear is never going to lead to them overcoming that fear. Hence, when you do that, you are writing someone a prescription for a life with an eating disorder. Rather, recovery should be about helping people to find the path to a life *without* an eating disorder. Why would we settle for anything less when we know that full recovery is absolutely possible?

Full recovery means no fear response to manage because the fear has gone.

It was a real game changer for me to be able to see how my fear presented itself. It presented as anger, avoidance, running away, pretending to eat, and inability to make decisions. You can only manage and overcome fear if you can understand how it presents. People with eating disorders are intelligent, resourceful, impressively able to tolerate discomfort, and above all else, we are stubborn as shit. Never underestimate a person with an eating disorder's ability to overcome fear. We are genetically gifted with all the necessary skills in order to be very good at rewiring fear responses if we decide to do it.

CHAPTER FOUR - HOW TO REWIRE FEAR OF WEIGHT GAIN

Alright! We've spent three chapters outlining what fear of weight gain is, how you got it, what it looks like, and why you need to rewire it. Now for the part where we discuss *how* you rewire it.

This won't take that long. It's really bloody simple. The way that you teach your brain not to be afraid of something that is afraid of is by doing the thing that you are afraid of, over and over again, until your brain has learnt not to fear it. If you want to teach your brain not to fear flying, you have to get in an airplane, over and over again. If you want to teach your brain not to fear snakes, you have to go and touch a snake, over and over again. If you want to teach your brain not to fear public speaking, you have to do a lot of public speaking. If you want to teach your brain not to fear weight gain, you have to do all the things you are afraid might lead to weight gain, over and over. You have to eat the foods that you have been restricting in unrestricted amounts. You have to trash your food rules. You have to stop compulsive movement. You have to stop purging. If you consistently act as if you are not afraid of weight gain by doing all the things that you are afraid of doing, you will rewire fear of weight gain.

Your brain learns from your actions. Every single time you restrict food, you are acting as if weight gain is something to be afraid of. You can't teach your brain that weight gain is nothing to be afraid of while acting as if you are afraid of weight gain. If you consistently act as if you have no fear of weight gain, and eat as if you have no fear of weight gain, and rest as if you have no fear of weight gain, your brain will learn not to fear weight gain.

This concept applies to everyone regardless of your level of fear of weight gain and how long you have had it. It doesn't even matter how you came to be at this point. The rewiring method is the same.

YOU'VE GOTTA TOUCH THE SNAKE

I'll flush this out some more. Let's use the snake example:

If you have a fear of snakes, and you no longer want to have a fear of snakes, how do you overcome your fear of snakes?

The answer is you go find a snake and you force yourself to pet it, over and over, until you cease to have a fear response upon touching the snake. Unfortunately, we can't talk ourselves out of fear. It isn't enough to simply say *"I don't want to be afraid of snakes anymore."* Nope, you gotta go and touch the snake.

Touching the snake is the only path to not being afraid of the snake. When you touch the snake and nothing bad happens to you, your brain has a data point referencing that the snake did not bite you. If you keep touching the snake and it keeps not biting you, these data points in favour of the snake being safe add up. At some point, you have enough data showing your brain that the snake is safe, that your brain stops deeming a HPA-axis fear response as appropriate. Rewired.

Now, because your brain is afraid of snakes, your brain will try and weasel its way out of touching the snake. It will try and find a different path. It will probably lead you up a load of garden paths actually in an attempt to not touch the snake. It will tell you that maybe hypnosis will work. Or maybe talk therapy will work. Or maybe just trying to think your way out of your fear of snakes will work. Anything, anything at all, just don't make me touch the snake. Ultimately, the only way that you can really overcome a fear response is by directly and personally doing the thing that you are afraid of. You can't sidestep this process. If I knew of a different or easier way that effectively works to rewire fear, I'd tell you. Unfortunately I don't, and you have to do it the old-fashioned way of ... actually doing it. But, on the plus side, I promise that overcoming your fear will make you an even more badass person than you already are. It is so worth it. Overcoming fear can be exhilarating and it can make you feel very powerful.

EXPECT TO BE AFRAID

So, you've made the decision that you are going to find a snake and touch it in order to overcome your fear of snakes. Do you expect to walk up to that snake tank and have zero fear?

No. Just the opposite: you would expect yourself to be utterly petrified! You're anticipating being very fearful when you touch the snake and you are prepping yourself for a big surge of fear when you actually do it. You're mentally preparing yourself to be ready to override the urge to turn and run out of the room. Anticipating and being ready for your fear response is key to overcoming it. It is important in eating disorder recovery that you expect those fear emotions — guilt, shame, disgust, etc, — so that when they come (which they will) you are ready to override them.

Luckily, by now, you are already probably pretty well acquainted with those fear-response emotions of guilt, shame, and disgust when you do things such as eat more than usual. You can use this familiarity to your advantage. You know when and where these emotions are likely to pop up so there is no excuse for being taken by surprise by them. It's not as if you didn't already know that as soon as you were done eating that huge slice of cake the guilt emotion would show up. It always does. Be ready for it. *Bring it on guilt, I double dog dare you.*

For whatever reason, a lot of people make the decision to recover and then are surprised that they feel that whopping smack of shame when they start to eat more or stop exercising. Well ... duh! Of course you will! Of course your brain is going to throw negative emotions at you if you do something that could lead to weight gain because your brain is afraid of weight gain and doesn't want you to do it. That's just your brain doing it's job. That's a healthy, well-working, non-defective fear response. And it isn't going to go away until fear of weight gain is rewired. So, be ready. Expect the guilt and shame and disgust that comes after eating. Identify it when it comes. Say to yourself *"yep, as expected, there is the guilt!"* Then push it aside and keep eating. Remember, you *can* override fear. You did that every time you got into bed despite the bed-monsters as a kid. You do it every time you face something in your life that you want to run away from. You are practiced at this!

The act of *not* reacting to the fear emotions your brain throws out that are designed to deter you from doing things that could lead to weight gain is a teaching point for your brain. Your lack of engagement with the guilt emotion will signal to your brain that perhaps guilt is no longer the relevant emotion in this situation. Additionally, your action of continuing to eat without restriction will drive it home to your brain that fear of weight gain is redundant — because your brain is watching you ignore the guilt and continue to eat.

GO BIG!

This part is counterintuitive, but I think it is important to consider.

If you're going to choose a snake to go and pet, you might be tempted to choose something puny — such as a little grass snake — because it feels less scary. Whatever, it's still a snake, right? You'll psych yourself up to go and touch this grass snake, and small as it is, you will still have a fear reaction to deal with. It may be a little snake but it's still a snake, and your brain will use the emotion of fear to warn you off it. Nonetheless, you work through that fear reaction and that takes energy and effort but you deal with it and you keep touching that little grass snake until your fear response ceases. Great. Well done.

Trouble is, just about any snake you come across that is bigger than a grass snake will still scare you. By choosing the least scary snake you could find, you only rewired your fear response to relatively small and un-scary snakes. You realise this, and you decide to step it up a notch and choose a slightly bigger snake. You go through the same process again. Having the fear response. Touching the snake until you have overcome it. You conquer your fear of that snake. Then, you step it up again for a slightly bigger snake. Have fear response. Deal with it. And so on. Every time you step it up, you have to go through the process over again.

Overcoming a fear response is mentally depleting. It takes energy and effort. Starting with a small snake and stepping up to bigger snakes means that you are having to go through this mentally exhausting experience over and over again. This is something a lot of people do in eating disorder recovery. They feel it makes sense to start small, and work up to bigger fear foods or situations. I can totally see why they think it would work better to approach recovery that way, but the reality is that constantly having to work through a fear response every time they step up almost always leads to burnout.

Alternatively, if you want to rewire your fear of snakes, you could go right for petting the biggest, scariest, and ugliest snake you can find. If you tackle the scariest snake first, you will only have to work through your fear response once, because just about every other snake you come across will look like an earthworm in comparison. This way you only have to do the hard work one time, then you are coasting. This is the equivalent of starting off by eating the biggest, gooiest, cheesiest burger you can find (without compensating). If you hit your biggest fear foods first, everything else will feel easy afterwards.

It seems like stepping up gradually should make things easier but it doesn't. All it does is exhaust you and make you feel like the need to micromanage your fear response will never end. This is one of the reasons why people burn out in recovery. Managing fear is tiring. You will save yourself a lot and make your chances of success greater the more you can condense the work you have to do. Touch the python. Start with the cake. Conquer the big mountains first and don't waste your energy running up hills.

TL;DR: Stepping up gradually is a trap. The cumulative effect of the effort of rewiring all those small fear responses is more exhausting in the long run than going big and hard at the start and having everything after that feel relatively easy.

GO ALL IN

In the same vein as the point above about going big, you need to go "all in." This is because unlike snakes, your fear of weight gain triggers are around you, all the time. So are your fear of weight gain reinforcers such as restriction, compulsive movement, and purging. It is tempting to pick one reinforcer at a time. You might decide to focus on eating without restriction first and tell yourself you will deal with stopping compulsive movement at a later date. The problem here is that compulsive movement reinforces and confirms your fear of weight gain, hence, all the while you are putting in all that effort with unrestricted eating, you are also still actively reinforcing the very fear belief system you are trying to rewire by continuing with compulsive movement.

You can't rewire a fear you are actively reinforcing. If you are reinforcing fear of weight gain with compulsive movement, fear of weight gain can't go away. That's like trying to teach your brain that you are not afraid of the snake whilst you are screaming and running away from the snake. Your brain isn't stupid (at least, I hope it isn't), it isn't going to believe you that weight gain is nothing to be afraid of when you are still acting as if you are afraid of weight gain by engaging in compulsive movement or restriction. Is it?

So all that work you are doing and all that effort you are putting in with your unrestricted eating still isn't going to result in the neural rewiring you need for full recovery, because you can't rewire a fear you are actively reinforcing.

Picking one thing at a time to work on sounds appealing, but the reality is that you burn out from a never-ending game of whack-a-mole. It doesn't get easier and your fear of weight gain doesn't reduce because you are still actively reinforcing it. At some point you will tap out, declare that recovery doesn't work for you, and jack it in. Nobody can do this work indefinitely because it is mentally knackering.

Yes, once again, I'm going to tell you that you have to take the harder path. You can't make it easier by picking one behaviour at a time to work on. You have to do them all at once. And you can hate me all you want for this, but I think you know I'm right. No whack-a-mole. It doesn't get you anything other than exhausted. Go all in. Do it all at once. Stop compulsive movement, stop all compensating or purging, and start unrestricted eating. Cease doing anything at all that reinforces fear of weight gain. Scary as shit, I know, but it is the most direct path and you will begin to see a difference in your fear levels within weeks of starting.

CONSISTENCY IS KEY

By design, your brain is suspicious of anything that tries to tell it not to be afraid of something it is afraid of. For this reason, if you want to convince your brain not to be afraid of something, you have to be very consistent with that message. If you work up the guts to touch the snake one time but run out of the room screaming the second time, you won't rewire anything. As far as your brain is concerned, you turning tail and running confirms what it knew all along—snakes are scary.

This is why you can't do that thing where you eat without restriction in the evening then get up the next morning and restrict. You are not rewiring shit if you do this. Whatever rewiring good you did the night before you just about undid when you started restricting again because restriction reinforces fear of weight gain. Your brain will see you restrict and think *"Yep, I knew it, weight gain is a threat after all."*

Again, dealing with a fear response is tiring. The more you can consolidate your effort, the best chance you have of not running out of steam before fear of weight gain is rewired. If you commit to consistently acting as if you are *not* afraid of weight gain, you will be surprised at how good your brain is at learning that weight gain is not a threat.

There is nothing dysfunctional about your brain when you have an eating disorder. Therefore, if rewiring fear of weight gain doesn't seem to be working, you need to look for how you are still inadvertently reinforcing the idea that weight gain is a threat to you with your actions. Where are you restricting? Where are you still following food rules? Where are you still engaging in compulsive movement? Ask yourself the questions that you want to avoid and you will see where you are reinforcing rather than rewiring.

DO IT YOUR WAY

Now that you know a lot of recovery is about overcoming fear, have a think about what works best for you when you are challenging your fear response.

Personally, if I were going to go touch a snake, I wouldn't take anyone with me. I'd go alone and do it alone because that is how I best deal with difficult situations. Having someone else with me would feel like a pressure. Whenever I have had to do something tricky and important in my life, I have preferred to do it alone. Sometimes this tendency of mine is troublesome, but it is what it is.

Other people might do it the opposite way and prefer to take a friend with them, because unlike me, having another person along feels like support rather than pressure. Some people might throw a snake-touching party and invite all their friends. There is no "right way" to rewire fear, there is only the way that feels best to you. You may choose to tackle fear of weight gain alone, or you may choose to involve your loved ones or a professional. Do whichever is going to make you the most successful. And if whatever you are doing isn't working, change it.

You are the best person to know how to manage the project of rewiring fear of weight gain. You know your fear response really well by now. You know where it comes up. You know how it tries to convince you not to do the things you are afraid of. You know the thought patterns it produces. You know the excuses it uses. You know the science studies it loves to quote because they align with and justify the fear. You know the memories it chooses to focus on because they reinforce the idea that restriction is the right choice. You know your fear, and all this information is exactly what you are going to use to overcome your fear.

KEEP IT SIMPLE

Fear confuses and complicates. If you are afraid of something, the simplest of things can seem complicated because your brain is looking for potential problems and reasons not to continue. Fear causes us to question and doubt. This is an effective safety function, and overall not a bad thing because it might be what causes you to double check that your parachute is working before you jump out of a plane.

Unfortunately, it is also the mechanism that makes trying to choose between a bakewell tart and a flapjack feel absolutely impossible when you have an eating disorder. In order to avoid becoming paralyzed with indecision and inertia, we need to be able to override the confusion and complication elements of fear. We can do that by recognising that if something seems complicated, we are likely having a fear response, and therefore need to take an action that will move us out of our sympathetic nervous system and into our parasympathetic nervous system. Asking yourself a question can have the effect of making you use the "thinking" part of your brain rather than the reactionary part of your brain. And I have just the question for times like this …

When your brain is feeling stuck I want you to ask yourself this one simple question: *"What action could I take in this moment that would best show my brain that I am not fearful of weight gain?"*

When you ask yourself that question, the answer becomes suddenly ridiculously clear: Obviously you should eat both the bakewell tart and the flapjack. Duh.

Recognising when your fear is causing things to seem more complicated than they really are is another important aspect of overcoming fear. Confusion causes hesitation. Learn to look out for it, and be ready to push yourself to act in a way that is pro-recovery as soon as you notice you are stalling.

FINAL POINTERS ON REWIRING
FEAR OF WEIGHT GAIN:

1. Anticipate and prepare for your fear response and you won't get sucked into it.
2. Actively seek out things that scare you — high-fat foods, rest, not exercising, not purging, etc. — and force yourself to do them until your fear response is eliminated.
3. Stop doing anything that reinforces fear of weight gain. This includes restricting, exercising, purging, food rules, and indulging in thought patterns around fear of weight gain, among many other things.
4. The more consistent you are with taking actions to rewire fear of weight gain, the faster the rewiring process will happen.

Remember: your brain is highly trainable and is a product of your own creation. There is nothing defective going on with your brain. It is simply responding to something it has been taught is a threat to it with a very functional fear response designed to keep you away from threats. This is a training issue, not a defect. Which is great news, because it is well within your capabilities to train your brain not to fear weight gain.

Doing this work of overcoming and rewiring fear will not only serve you for recovery. It will leave you with a skillset that will serve you in many situations in life. Not many people have the opportunity to work on overcoming such a strong level of fear. I always say to people *"if you can do recovery, you can do anything."* This is because achieving full recovery from a restrictive eating disorder requires us to be so many things: determined, strong-willed, stubborn, focused ... and brave. I never met a person with an eating disorder who wasn't able to be all these things — it must be part of the genetic package. I've known enough people with eating disorders to know that you — yes, I'm talking to *you* — can do this.

Teaching your brain not to fear weight gain will give you so much more than you anticipate. It is crucial for your recovery, but It will also change your relationship with your body. It will alter the way you feel about and respect your body. Your body is the only thing that will be with you every second of every day of your life. You *have* to get along with your body if you want to be happy in life. I found that by overcoming fear of weight gain, I was able to fully let go and allow my body to *be* ... and this is a fantastic freedom. I sincerely hope that you will soon experience it.

CHAPTER FIVE - FOR PROFESSIONALS WORKING IN THIS FIELD

Eating disorder professionals are just as susceptible to fear of weight gain and fatphobia imposed by our culture as anyone else is. This can be very problematic. If an eating disorder professional does not confront and overcome their biases before they start working with people in recovery, they risk worsening rather than bettering their clients' chances of success.

Due to our cultural belief systems around bodyweight, most people (including healthcare professionals) see a degree of restriction as normal — even, dare I say, "healthy." They also see their tendency to view larger bodies as undesirable as normal and justified. Hence, when an eating disorder dietician or therapist says to their client *"Okay, I think your weight is good now, you can cut back on your eating a little,"* they don't hear the instructions to restrict coming out of their mouths, and they don't understand the psychological disruption they cause.

Implicit bias is a bitch to deal with due to the unconscious nature of it. However, if you want to work as a counsel to a specific population, I believe you have a duty to explore any implicit biases you may have that are particularly relevant to that population. Fear of weight gain, fatphobia, "good"/"bad" food judgements, and thin bias are a few that spring to mind for anyone interested in working with eating disorders..

If an eating disorder professional's own fear of weight gain and/or fatphobia goes unaddressed, they are a liability when working with people in recovery from eating disorders. This is because, at some point sooner or later, their fear of weight gain is going to show itself when they are addressing their client. It may be directed towards themselves. It may be directed towards the client. It will never go unnoticed by the client. It will always cause confusion, disillusionment, and doubt.

Here are some examples:

- "You are now weight restored"
- "It's great that you can eat full-fat yoghurt. I have stick to low-fat myself"
- "I think we can reduce your meal plan now, as you are weight restored"
- "Your weight is back in the healthy range, so now we need to just maintain rather than gain any more"
- "Great, well we are at the point where we can start removing some of those extra snacks"
- "You can cut back a bit now, we don't want you to go over your target weight too much"
- "Okay, so now we are at the stage where you need to make healthier food choices, so you don't continue to gain weight."
- "Time to start swapping out full-fat milk for semi-skimmed. Pretty much all people use semi-skimmed or skimmed milk. That's more normal"

The above are all actual statements that eating disorder treatment providers (dietitians and therapists) have said to people in recovery. They all reek of a treatment provider who is 1) afraid of weight gain, and 2) doesn't trust the body to manage its food intake and weight. This is a huge problem in this industry, because these are the two biggest belief systems that a person with an eating disorder needs to rewire in order to fully recover.

The *"You are now weight restored"* one really cracks me up. The sheer arrogance of that sort of statement. As if they hold the authority on when another person's body is weight restored. The only thing that has the authority to decide when a person is fully nutritionally rehabilitated is that person's own body. Anyone else's opinion is just their opinion, and it is usually an opinion that is filtered through that person's own fear of weight gain and fatphobia as impressed on them by our thin-obsessed culture.

How can a person with an eating disorder rewire their own distrust of their body when their treatment providers are acting as if their charts and textbooks know more about their body than their body does? As I outlined in *Rehabilitate, Rewire, Recover!*, the body will tell us when it is nutritionally rehabilitated by decreasing mental hunger. Until that happens, a person is not nutritionally rehabilitated — regardless of what their weight is. The treatment provider's judgement over what a person's weight should be and when they should be nutritionally rehabilitated has no place in this discussion at all. The body is the guide.

"It's great that you can eat full-fat yoghurt. I have to stick to low-fat myself," is an example of the treatment provider referring to and normalising their own dietary restriction. While unfortunately it may be true that most people in our culture restrict food, this certainly is not desirable, nor will it lead someone to full recovery. It is not helpful to a person in recovery to hear that their treatment provider engages in restriction — the very person who is supposed to be helping them recover.

If there is truth to the statement that most people use semi-skimmed or skimmed milk over full-fat, all that does is show how messed up and fearful people are over their weight, and how little we understand our bodies. Using semi-skimmed milk over full-fat milk in your tea or on your breakfast cereal isn't going to make an iota of difference to anything. Suggesting that it does is acting as if the body is that sensitive to fat that an amount that tiny could make a difference — that is honestly the last thing a person with an eating disorder needs to hear as they already fear that this is true. It is not true. If your body is at its natural unsuppressed bodyweight, you can vary what you eat quite significantly and your body will stay within that range. Our bodies are intelligent organisms; let's not insult them with the notion that using full-fat milk in your latte can't be handled.

A primary characteristic of many eating disorders is orthorexia. So how can anyone who calls themself an "Eating Disorder Specialist" not understand that saying something like, *"Okay, so now we are at the stage where you need to make healthier food choices, so you don't continue to gain weight,"* is going to send their client reeling backwards? That's like telling someone with contamination OCD that their fingernails look dirty and there might be germs on the couch they are sitting on. It would be laughable if it weren't a statement that I happen to know started a client into a 3-year relapse.

How about *"Great, well we are at the point where we can start removing some of those extra snacks"*? Ouch! That stings. As a person who once had an eating disorder and knowing how very hungry I was before, during, and after my initial weight gain in recovery, I know this one would have felt like a slap in the face. Imagine that you are eating your (probably massively inadequate) meal plan and you are still hungry pretty much all of the time. Then your dietitian goes and tells you that you need to eat less because you have gained weight. How confusing is that? How dismissive is it of your body's hunger signals? How does this teach you anything other than it is your weight that guides how much you are allowed to eat? It confirms the thought *"I only get to eat what I want if I am underweight."* Again, by this statement, the treatment provider has caused all sorts of doubt and confusion by acting as if restriction is normal unless one is underweight.

Anyone who says anything such as *"Great, well we are at the point where we can start removing some of those extra snacks"* needs to be removed from treating people with eating disorders — especially if they don't understand what is wrong with that statement and how it is damaging. This is precisely why I use the word *liability* when talking about some treatment professionals, because many people are so unaware of their own fear of weight gain and restrictive doctrine when it comes to food and eating and bodyweight that they have no idea the chaos they create when they open their mouths.

If you're a treatment provider and you know you have said anything similar to the examples I put in the bullet points above, you should not be working with people with eating disorders until you have thoroughly addressed your own fear of weight gain and fatphobia. Even if you can't see your own fear of weight gain, and even if you don't believe you have it, if you have said any of those things I promise you that you do. As soon as you allow your own fear of weight gain to enter into your client sessions, you are a detriment to your client's recovery.

Fear of weight gain is a product of the implicit bias that our culture has that implies that thin is good and fat is not. It is not your fault that you have fear of weight gain, we all do. It is, however, your responsibility to address your implicit bias if you want to work with people with eating disorders. Doing the work to address fear of weight gain can be uncomfortable, ugly, and empowering. It can take a long time, and it likely means that you will change as a person, so don't rush it. Do the work and do it properly, or go and work with a different section of the population. Do not inflict your fear of weight gain on your clients.

[1] Ekman P (1992) An argument for basic emotions. Cogn Emotion 6:169–200

[2] LeDoux JE (1996) The Emotional Brain (Simon and Schuster, New York)

[3] Davis M (1992) The role of the amygdala in conditioned fear. The Amygdala: Neurobiological Aspects of Emotion, Memory, and Mental Dysfunction, ed Aggleton JP (Wiley-Liss, New York), pp 255–306

[4] LeDoux JE (1996) The Emotional Brain (Simon and Schuster, New York)

[5] Bornemann B, Winkielman P, van der Meer E (2012) Can you feel what you do not see? Using internal feedback to detect briefly presented emotional stimuli. Int J Psychophysiol 85(1):116–124.

[6] Hariri AR, (2002) The amygdala response to emotional stimuli: A comparison of faces and scenes. Neuroimage 17(1):317–323

[7] LeDoux JE(1984) Cognition and emotion: Processing functions and brain systems. Handbook of Cognitive Neuroscience, ed Gazzaniga MS (Plenum, New York), pp 357–368.

[8] Emotions as higher-order states of consciousness. Joseph E. LeDoux, Richard Brown Proceedings of the National Academy of Sciences Mar 2017, 114 (10) E2016-E2025; DOI: 10.1073/pnas.1619316114

Printed in Great Britain
by Amazon

62714069R00045